NOW, WHAT DO I DO?

By:

PASTOR LOUIS THOMAS, SR.

House of Bread Publishing
Picayune, MS

House of Bread Publishing
1190 South Beech Street
Picayune, Mississippi 39466
Copyright © 2017 by House of Bread Publishing

First Paperback edition February 2017

Manufactured in the United States of America

Scriptures referred to in this book are taken from the most up to date translation of the Holy Bible published by Zondervan Publishing House and provided online by biblegateway.com.

ISBN-13:
978-0692834251 (House of Bread Publishing)

ISBN-10:
0692834257

<u>DEDICATION</u>

I dedicate this book to two important ladies in my life: the first is Ann Elizabeth Thomas my mother, the great lessons you taught and how they resonated in my heart from youth to adulthood. I learned from you it's not how people treat you but how you treat yourself that will determine how you treat others. I thank you for your firm hand when you weren't at all bashful in pulling my coat tail and reminding me during the most critical period of my life, when I was about to emotionally fall to pieces, *"You are God's anointed"*. Those words rocked me back on the straight and narrow and strengthened me for the rest of the journey. Thanks, Mom, for rescuing me from spiritual catastrophe. I was always under your watchful eye, even at a distance. I'm sure you have untold stories you could share. I thank God that He has allowed you to see the reality of what HE has called me to do materialize. My prayer is, when you read this book, it brings a deeper love for GOD and a commitment to never take your eyes off the LORD GOD ALMIGHTY.

Love you so much.

The second lady is my wife Alma K. Thomas, the in the background work horse that helped plow the row of the gospel field with me, who caught the vision GOD gave me and never lost interest, who sharpens me when I feel dull, strengthens me with GOD'S Word when I have given out all, and comforts me with encouraging words from on high. Kaye, sometimes you may feel unappreciated, but know that I thank GOD for you, for your presence has been nothing but a great blessing. Your Christian character radiate the beauty of the LORD. Continue to serve the MASTER and I'm assured at the end of your journey there's a crown waiting. Love you just as much.

FORWORD

Internal pressure can cause a person to buckle under. For me it happened when I worked for a major government contractor, and everyone but me was laid off in my department. One lady attended and worked in church faithfully; a man had all the educational credentials, but they kept me. I could not understand why I was chosen, and the pressure landed me at church—not just any church but a church under the leadership of Rev. Louis Thomas, Sr. That was over 25 years ago.

Pastor Thomas started regular Bible study; I was not accustomed to that, but I soaked up every word. Awhile back I came across notes I took during that time where he taught us the three p's of worship: praise, prayer, and I am not too sure about that third "p"; but it has to be preaching the Word of God because that is what Pastor Thomas has done ever since I have been under his tutelage.

My life has changed thanks to Pastor Thomas's teaching. Eventually I *was* laid off also and ended up on government assistance for several years; however, thanks to my praising the Lord Jesus and praying to the Master, I did not stay on government assistance. Through Pastor's teachings, I learned that there was truly nothing too impossible for God and went back to first a community college then to a university for which through the grace of God, I received several degrees.

I can testify that those sweet "p's" of worship that Pastor Thomas was the first to introduce me to have helped me through many situations: death of parents, making ends meet, sicknesses, stress on the job, and any other problematic situation. In situations that would have had the potential to knock me off my feet didn't because I knew the value of praising the Lord no matter the circumstance through prayer and by hearing the Word of God. Any given Sunday or Tuesday Night Bible Study, Pastor Thomas may throw out a Bible nugget like "let God fight your battles" which would apply directly to me. These kind of nuggets are worth their weight in gold which is why I hate to miss church.

It would behoove anyone to hear what this man of God has to say; I am positive that his message will be life changing to all that hear what he has to say. I congratulate you Pastor Thomas on this endeavor and potential to help thousands of readers just like your teachings have helped me.

Virena B. Simmons

Have you ever wondered, "How do I recover from a spiritual decline"? Are you looking for, or are you in desperate need for a renovation of the heart? A transformation of Spirit? This is the book for you! It is vitally important as you read this book that you capture the abundant Hope, Strength, Peace, Guidance, and the Wisdom of God printed on every page.

The Author, Pastor Louis Thomas, Sr., is a Pastor that truly lives, walks, Pastors, teaches, and preaches in the anointing of the Holy Spirit. He doesn't just tell you about the Christian life; he lives it. I'm reminded of the first time I heard Pastor Thomas teach at Bible Study, I was on the edge of my seat, totally drawn in and captivated by the powerful Words of God that he had spoken.

Pastor Thomas has captured what the Holy Spirit has inspired him to write on the pages of this book. I warn you now to get ready because you are about to be held hostage by this book titled, "Now, What Do I Do"?

Persuaded by the gospel and run down by the Church, this book invites you to take a closer look at life experiences and the choices you have lived through or made in the past. "Now, What Do I Do"? gives you a clear understanding of how to move forward in Christ. This book is a "must" read.

In fact, I'm absolutely convinced that this book will inspire and motivate you. Allow the words to resonate in your spirit.

Now, read this book! That's an order!

Dr. Dawn C. Haralson

I could never forget the moment that I first met Rev. Louis Thomas our author. He is a person that I as well as many other were easily drawn too. I found him to be one that was in love with God and someone who cares about the spirituality of God's people. Throughout the years that I have known him, I've seen the personal sacrifices and dedication that he has given to the study of God's word and his willingness to share unselfishly the many truths revealed as the Spirit of God opened up the Word to him.

Thomas as I often call him, has always been a man serious about kingdom building. It has always been amazing to me how just through plain old conversation he always has a timely word in season for all that he comes in contact with. He has a burden in his heart for the people of God, a strong desire to help people reach and maximize their full potential. Through our many conversations it has always been evident that he desired to be used of God and gives the best of his service.

Rev. Thomas is one that would make you think, while providing answers to many questions that we are often afraid to ask. This book is a product of the quality time that he has spent with our Lord with every intent to be a blessing to the readers. Throughout the years it has been a tradition in many Christian Circles to win souls but, then what happens after the baptism and communion. In the reading of these writings, I believe that you will find the answer to the *"What's Next."* Not only *"What's Next"* but he answers the *"How Too"*, how to move forward and grow in a manner that is consistent with the plans that our Heavenly Father has for each of us.

The word contained in this book will be a blessing to its many readers. Rev. Thomas, you have been a blessing in my life and through your diligent study and teaching of the word you have blessed many others however; God has granted you His favor and has inspired you to reach even greater masses. Thank you for helping so many take the next step.

Pastor Leonard E. Craft
Macedonia Baptist Church
Slidell, LA

This book written by my treasured friend of over twenty-five years in the ministry. Rev. Louis Thomas has captured the essence of what the Christian church should teach new members after they have become part of the body of Christ. Louis Thomas is a wordsmith. He uses words so clearly and cleverly as Vance Havner once stated "to comfort the afflicted and to afflict the comfortable". We truly should be training, teaching and empowering new members of the church to become life-long learners based on solid biblical principles. The Baptist church has done a good job over the years at bringing new members into the flock , but not as good a job tapping into all of that new energy and excitement. Pastor Thomas makes a strong case for equipping them once they are on the rolls. He makes it plain that God has a specific role for every Christian worker. Just as the human body has a distinct role for each of its parts, so does the body of Christ for each of its members. We are truly made up of many members, but one body in Christ. The "Great Commission" found in Matthew 28:19, 20 reminds us that after baptism we are to teach them to observe all things.

One of the key elements of the church's role is to teach, teach, and teach some more until every saint has been fully equipped in order to be able to withstand the wiles of the devil, and having done all to stand.

Rev. Louis Thomas has done an excellent job in laying out how we should help the new additions to be functional in their new church families and assets in the up-building of the kingdom of God. They should never be left to figure it out for themselves. This inspiring book should give impetus to pastors, laymen, new membership teachers and other Christian workers in the vineyard. This is an eye-opener for the church and should serve as a catalyst in providing support to new members.

Rev. Thomas Walters
Second New Light Baptist Church
New Orleans, LA

TABLE OF CONTENTS

INTRODUCTION

ABOUT THE AUTHOR

INTRODUCTION

If a restaurant advertises its business, provides the atmosphere for dining, and even offers a menu but had no food, how would you feel sitting in their dining area? This is the condition of many churches today, they advertise to be a hospital for sinners, a contact between heaven and earth, a place to feast on the word of God, but they don't always deliver. Jesus condemns such action.

Matthew 23:15 - "Woe unto you, scribes and Pharisees, hypocrites! For ye compass sea and land to make one proselyte, and when he is made, ye make him twofold more the child of hell than yourselves".

When the Lord God Almighty instructed me to begin this ministry He said, it shall be called *"The House of Bread", for it shall be the place where my people shall be nourished in my word.*

There must be growth after conversion; conversion is not the end of the matter, but the registration in which we enter the kingdom of God. What we now need is instructions on how to live kingdom lives pleasing to God!

This book takes rise out of that need, it is not intended to replace the Word of God, but alone with the Bible aid, the babe in Christ to find his/her way.

When I accepted Christ as my personal Savior, I needed instruction on how to live a life pleasing to God, but it appeared that I became lost in plain sight without any idea what to do on the Lord's program. I heard the gospel and responded by confessing and receiving Christ as Lord, I was baptized and given the right hand of fellowship, and the pastor looked me in the eyes and said, *"Find your place, get in your place, and stay in your place."*

At Saul's conversion he asked JESUS on the Damascus Road, *"What will thou have me to do?"* JESUS said, *"Go into the city and it shall be told thee what thou must do."* The city you must enter for instruction is the church filled with the presence of God.

Hebrews 10:25 - "Not forsaking the assembling of ourselves together, as the custom is with some".

Our minds must also be prepared to give heartfelt worship.

Psalm 100:4 – "Enter into his gates with thanksgiving, and into his courts with praise: be thankful unto him, and bless his name".

You will feel the presence of GOD when you enter the sanctuary so expect The LORD GOD to speak His will to your mind through His Living Word. It's vital for you to grasp, that out of this great sea of humanity, GOD hand-picked you to be His servant to bring glory to his Name representing heaven on earth.

It won't be a cats-walk, you will have opposition from the three great enemies of the soul; *the world, the flesh* and *the devil,* who will oppose you with a diabolical campaign to lead the babe (you) in CHRIST astray. Therefore, it is most vital that you be equipped with the Word of GOD to faithfully remain in CHRIST, put on the whole Armour of GOD, develop faith from the word of GOD to withstand the attacks and lead a successful campaign for GOD.

After some thirty years of ministering, preaching and teaching GOD'S Word, I noticed that the excitement of becoming a child of GOD is lost, because no one is telling the new believer where he/she fits in or what to do next after conversion. Allow me to say, first of all you are GOD'S *ekklesia,* His building, His tabernacle and you are responsible to faithfully submit to The HOLY SPIRIT of GOD and through the Word of GOD develop into the image of JESUS CHRIST the SON of the Living GOD.

Think of your Christian growth like a transition from high school to college. In high school, the teacher is on you about getting your homework done, paying attention in class and so on, but when you reach college no one makes you do anything. The expectation is that you should be self-motivated and driven. As a new born convert in CHRIST, just thinking about what he has done for you ought to motivate you to know Him more and more.

To develop into the image of CHRIST, sacrifices have to be made. Think about sacrifice as a diet, good carbs in and bad carbs out. The Word of GOD in and gossip, lies and ole wives tales out. Then think about sacrifices as determination. As the salmon swim upstream against fierce currents to spawn, as a child of GOD, you must be determined to go against the fierce currents of the pull of the world. The apostle Paul says, *"I will let nothing separate me from the love of GOD"* the words of our LORD to you is, *enter ye in at the strait gate, narrow is the way that leads to life.*

Let me strongly say with conviction, GOD has placed men and women alike to assist you in your developmental stages but it is up to you. No one will force JESUS on you. Your desire to become more like the LORD will be determined by your *drive, determination* and *desire.*

What the church has put on display has become a turn off to many. That which is holy is treated as common and that which is of the world is being offered to a HOLY GOD.

It is all lies. I believe that in the teachings, or a lack thereof, the church has become focused on earthly prosperity. It seems to have lost interest in making disciples and strengthening the body of CHRIST.

My prayer is, this book, by the grace of GOD and His HOLY SPIRIT guidance, would create a hunger within you so strong that you begin to feast on the word of GOD and it stirs you up to stand firm in the faith and to put boots on the ground to advance the kingdom of GOD among men.

Matthew 5:16 – "Let your light so shine before men, that they may see your good works, and glorify your Father which is in heaven".

Chapter One

DOES THE LORD REALLY KNOW YOU?

Matthew 7:22-23 – "Many will say to me in that day, Lord, Lord, have we not prophesied in thy name? And in thy name have cast out devils? And in thy name done many wonderful works? And then will I profess unto them, I never knew you: depart from me, ye that work iniquity".

Before we began, I want this to resonate with you - works without faith is dead and faith without works is just as dead [Jas.2:20].

There is a song that says, "May the works I've done speak for me".

I desire you grasp the words of the LORD JESUS:

John 10:14 - "I am the good shepherd, and know my sheep, and am known of mine".

John 10:3 - "The sheep hear his voice: and he calleth his own sheep by name, and leadeth them out".

In the above printed text, JESUS is talking about the in times, as He points to a particular event taking place at a particular while using the expression "in that day" which specifically points to the day of judgment when every person, dead or alive, will stand before ALMIGHTY GOD and give account of their stewardship of the things done in the body. It is in reference to that day, when night will lose its power to cover wrongdoings and sins will be exposed before He that sits upon the throne of judgment. In that day, when the mountains will give up every dead body that died on its slopes or down in its canyons. In that day, when the seas could no longer hold those who lost their lives in wars, or pleasure seekers looking for deep sea adventures. In that day, when the torment chambers of hell itself must give up those who refused to claim JESUS as LORD and died in their sins as enemies of GOD. In that day, which Solomon called [Prov. 6:34] "the day of vengeance"; Joel calls it [Joel 2:31] "a great and terrible day"; Malachi says, it will be [Mal. 4:5] "a dreadful day" and JESUS the Revelator says, [Rev. 6:17] it will be a "great day of His wrath". In that day, when no excuse will be given or accepted, no liar or lies will be spoken in His presence.

Paul says, [Rom. 2:1] "whosoever you are, thou art inexcusable" because that day the secrets of the heart will be exposed. JESUS says, in that day they shall call Him "Lord, Lord" they will be saying the right thing but got the wrong motive. JESUS said [Jn. 13:13] "You call me Master and LORD, and you're right to do so, cause that's what I am"; [Lk. 6:46b] "but you don't do the things which I say". They had a hallow sincerity, in other words, they were sincere in church attendance, giving tithes and offerings, prayer and preaching, teaching but it wasn't heart service.

Look at the Pharisee standing in the temple [Lk. 18:11] praying, JESUS says, <u>with himself</u>, "God, I thank you, that I am better than other men, I fast twice a day, I give tithes of all I possess". It was a prayer of selfishness as the Pharisee stood before The MOST HIGH GOD and boasted about what he done and not one time said anything about what the LORD GOD had done for him.

Like these individuals in our text, it was a service rendered to be seen of men. Notice <u>they said</u>, they prophesy, in other words, they foretold events and spoke under inspiration, they ejected demons and done many mighty works, in His name. Oh, how many today are using His name, wearing His name, talking about His name but don't have a real conversion in His name! It's by our faith in JESUS CHRIST as LORD that we are made acceptable to GOD, cleansed by His blood, robed in His righteousness and made new through His resurrection.

Paul writes [2 Tim. 1:12b] "For I know whom I have believed, and am persuaded that He is able to keep that which I have committed unto Him against that day"; then he says, "I stand confident in the promises GOD made" [2 Tim.4:8] "Henceforth there is laid up for me a crown of righteousness, which the Lord the Righteous Judge, shall give me at that day and not to me only, but unto all them that love His appearing".

There will be some surprises at the judgment seat of CHRIST. JESUS says, [Matt. 7:21] "Not everyone that saith unto me, Lord, Lord, shall enter into the kingdom of heaven; but he that doeth the will of my Father which is in heaven". The apostle John says, here is His will [1 Jn. 3:23] "And this is his commandment, that we should believe on the name of his Son Jesus Christ". Because they rejected JESUS as LORD and tried to get into the kingdom another way, <u>they wanted to be accepted by their works</u>. They were surprised their works were being rejected and not just their works, but they were being rejected because of everything they had done in His name. They were astounded that their names were not on the roll that would give them access into the Kingdom of GOD.

Here, the secrets of their hearts are exposed. These individuals believed that works made them acceptable to GOD; they banked everything they had on it and was confident their works would hold up and be acceptable before GOD.

Maybe they never received Paul's memo in [Eph. 2:9] "Not of works, lest any man should boast". JESUS said, "Then will I profess in front of everybody. I will tear off the mask and reveal your wolf mentality in sheep clothing, your acting on the world's stage, holy looking outwardly but full of dead men bones/filthy inwardly, using my name for your personal gain. I will profess before them, I never knew you".

When I was in high school, my friend Ricky one day during lunch break asked me, "Are you going with a certain girl?"

I responded, "No, I don't know this person; I don't even know what she looks like."

Then he began pressing saying, "You just don't want anybody to know you are dating this girl."

I continued in my defense, and finally began asking, "Well? Who is she?"

He interrupted my question by saying, "Here she comes now."

I looked in the direction he was looking and two young ladies were walking towards us. I asked him which one, and before I could get my question out, they were soon to pass by us and Ricky took one of the young ladies by the hand and asked her, "Don't you go with Louis?"

She said, "Yes, he's some kind of guy!"

I was quick to respond, "I have never even met you! I don't even know you! If I have never met you, how then can we be going together?"

This is important - it's necessary that you know the LORD but it's vital that He knows you! Here's the question, does the LORD really know you?

Well, let me tell you about me. The LORD knows me from that day of conversion when I confessed Him LORD before all, when He offered through the gospel to take my sins and cleanse me of all my filthiness and unrighteousness, and I accepted His offer. I believed Him to be the MESSIAH, the LAMB of GOD who takes away the sins of the world. The ONLY BEGOTTEN SON of ALMIGHTY GOD, through Him only is salvation made available to a sinner like you and me. He knows me, from that day in baptism, when I shared His death and the old man was buried completely out of sight in a liquid grave. Then, He knows me in His resurrection, when the HOLY SPIRIT raised me to new life and my LORD wrapped me in His righteous character.

Does the LORD really know you? Did you meet Him through the gospel at the cross, where His glorious light first sprang forth like the dawning of a new day and your gloom turned to joy? He died for you, from the sixth to the ninth hour. Stars couldn't stand the sight and they fainted and fell from their silver sockets and the moon's grief was so intense that its tears became blood as it dripped away in blood. They placed JESUS our LORD in Joseph's new tomb three full days and three full nights. He laid hidden away from sight. But early the first day of the week He rose with all power.

It's not enough that you know Him be sure, be very sure He really knows you. If you accepted GOD'S gift of His only Begotten SON, then rest assured He knows your name!

Ephesians 2:9 - "Not of works, lest any man should boast".

John 10:1 - "Verily, verily, I say unto you, he that entereth not by the door into the sheepfold, but climbeth up some other way, the same is a thief and a robber".

Chapter Two

LET'S GET STARTED

Matthew 6:33a - "But seek ye first the kingdom of God".

Let's begin with the understanding that your salvation is personal, between you and GOD. It is not between you and your neighbor, you and your family or friends, but you and GOD. When you get it right, only then you can help others get it right.

Matthew 7:5 - "First cast out the beam out of thine own eye, and then shalt thou see clearly to cast the mote out of thy brother's eye".

In the above scripture the word "seek" is present tense which carries the idea of continuation; therefore, this seeking comes with a desire of the heart to claim the thing you seek. Jesus gave an analogy of this in the parable of the lost coin [Lk. 15:8-10]. The woman had ten coins and lost one. JESUS says she lit a candle and swept the house and searched diligently until she found the coin. Let your searching be with the heart and a determination to never give up until you find what you seek regardless of what it is and how long it takes. JESUS said,

Matthew - 18:3 - "Except ye be converted, and become as little children, ye shall not enter into the kingdom of heaven".

The disciples were arguing amongst themselves and they came to JESUS to settle the argument of who shall be the greatest in the kingdom of heaven. JESUS called a little child, as exhibit A, to teach an important lesson. Before you can talk about being great in the kingdom, make sure you get in the kingdom.

This is how you get in the kingdom. Please notice, the LORD <u>called</u> the child and the child <u>responded</u>. First, conversion doesn't take place until you respond to the Master's call through the gospel.

Hebrews 3:7-8a - "Wherefore (as the Holy Ghost saith, To day if ye will hear his voice, harden not your hearts".

You must become as little children, which speaks of <u>humility</u>. We're given a clear view of this in the words of our LORD. JESUS said, [Matt. 19:24] "it is easier for a camel to go through the eye of a needle (with a hump), than for a rich man to enter into the kingdom of God (with his pride)". So if you're going to enter the kingdom, you must trade your heavy burdens for the yoke of The LORD JESUS.

The gospel is the mirror that the man of God holds up so you could see what you look like before a HOLY GOD. The apostle Paul says, [Rom. 1:16] he holds up this mirror because "for it is the power of God unto salvation to everyone that believeth". The gospel of CHRIST shows you the spiritual cancer in your life that needs to go! The first thing the gospel does, when you read it, is make you humble. Consider this: the first thing the camel would have to do to get through the eye of the needle, was to get down on its knees. Then, whatever load it was carrying, his master would strip it off. Once you get humble before GOD, you then acknowledge that you're bearing a heavy load of sin that will prevent you from entering the kingdom: the hump of hate, puffed up pride, the load of envy, full of jealousy, self, and selfishness, all which need to fit through the narrow passage of the kingdom. So it is imperative that you are stripped.

Paul says, [Rom. 10:9a] "if thou wilt confess" confession is the stripping process that prepares you for the HOLY GHOST filling. In other words, repentance brings you to a point where all charges are dropped; every accusation made against you will be looked at as insufficient evidence and will not be brought up again against you. The camel still had to struggle to get in the needle's eye; he would struggle and wiggle a long time trying to get through the needle's eye, he would get bumped, bruised and scarred but he wouldn't quit. The camel was determined. <u>How bad do you want to get in the kingdom of GOD?</u> When I played sports I wanted to win, I wanted to win so bad I could taste it.

Do you want the kingdom so bad you could taste it?

Psalm 34:8 - "O taste and see that the Lord is good".

It's going to take <u>focus</u> and <u>determination</u>! As you travel this road while bearing a cross and seeing a traveler every now and then, there is no doubt that you are going to get bumped and bruised; you're going to get your feelings hurt. Are you willing to wiggle? Wiggling means struggling and struggling carries the idea of combat, combat from a Christian point of view. Meaning, you may very well be cussed out by those you bless, hated for showing love, persecuted for shining a light in dark lives but you must remain faithful to The LORD who commissioned you to spread the gospel. Are you willing? If you are, then let's get started.

The first thing you should understand is, the kingdom is not being offered to you because of who you are or what you've done; it is for GOD'S own glory.

Psalm 15:1 - "Not unto us, but unto thy name give glory".

You seek GOD believing and knowing who He is, and that He is a rewarder of them who diligently seek him [Heb. 11:6]. The beginning of our walk starts with a genuine conversion which includes repentance and faith; repentance involves the heart being affected by the gospel of CHRIST and genuinely turning from sin, and faith involves the heart genuinely turning to GOD. The real you is unveiled in your conversion and you see exactly what you look like from GOD'S point of view, Isaiah exclaimed,

Isaiah 6:5 - "Woe is me! For I am undone; because I am a man of unclean lips, and I dwell in the midst of a people of unclean lips: for mine eyes have seen the King, the Lord of hosts".

Job saw himself [Job 40:4a] "I am vile" disgustedly filthy and the apostle Paul called himself [Rom. 7:24] "wretched man" trapped in a body of death. The real you, the true man of the heart, is only visible in a genuine conversion. Deliverance is made available by confessing what you are.

Jesus asked the man in Gadarene [Lk.8] "What is your name?"

He said, "Legion. I'm full of demons."

Jesus said, "Come out of the man!"

An Angel wrestled with Jacob on the bank of Jabbok he asked him, "What is your name?" [Gen. 32:27-28]

He said, "Jacob the schemer".

The Lord touched his thigh and said, "You shall no longer be called Jacob, but your new name shall be Israel, prince with GOD."

To get your spiritual transformation & deliverance, you must acknowledge CHRIST and truly confess what you are. What is your name? _____, alcoholic, drug addict, sinner, liar, adultery, backstabber, husband taker/wife snatcher? What is your name? And remember, do not say that you are not that bad, it IS really that bad! We don't measure our sins against the sins of others, we measure our sins (impurities) against the purity of JESUS CHRIST our LORD, JESUS said, [Matt. 9:12] "They that be whole need not a physician, but they that are sick."

Many people join a church without a genuine conversion and call themselves a Christian; you don't become a Christian on the terms you set. The church doesn't have the power to make you one, neither does just giving up bad habits. A Christian is an individual who shares the identity of Christ. That's what apostle Paul was expressing.

Galatians 2:20 - "I am crucified with Christ (identified in His death): nevertheless I live (identified in His resurrection); yet not I (no longer am I seen), but Christ liveth in me (but Christ is seen in me): and the life which I now live in the flesh I live by the faith of the Son of God (CHRIST is living out His life in me), who loved me, and gave himself for me".

It all begins with hearing the gospel of JESUS CHRIST. Once the true gospel is heard, it produces faith and brings a conviction which Strong Encyclopedia calls the first degree of repentance. The true gospel of GOD laid before us in the Bible unveils the true condition of mankind, shaped in iniquity.

[Ps. 51:5] "Behold, I was shapen in iniquity; and in sin did my mother conceive me", <u>alienated from the life of God</u>. [Eph. 4:18] "Having the understanding darkened, being alienated from the life of God through the ignorance that is in them, because of the blindness of their heart", <u>enemies</u> [Rom. 5:10] "For if, when we were enemies, we were reconciled to God by the death of his Son, much more, being reconciled, we shall be saved by his life", <u>sinful</u> [Rom. 3:23] "For all have sinned, and come short of the glory of God"; and <u>destined to eternal damnation</u> [Rev. 20:12-15] "And I saw the dead, small and great, stand before God; and the books were opened: and another book was opened, which is the book of life: and the dead were judged out of those things which were written in the books, according to their works. And the sea gave up the dead which were in it; and death and hell delivered up the dead which were in them: and they were judged every man according to their works. And death and hell were cast into the lake of fire. This is the second death. And whosoever was not found written in the book of life was cast into the lake of fire".

GOD sent His Only Begotten SON to offer Himself for man's salvation. He alone makes possible the forgiveness of sins. Acting as

MEDIATOR, He brings both GOD and man together.

John 3:16 – "For God so loved the world; that He gave his only begotten Son, that whosoever believeth in him should not perish, but have everlasting life".

John 1:12 - "But as many as received him, to them gave he power to become the sons of God, even to them that believe on his name".

Therefore, upon your hearing the gospel, it should bring a conviction. Being convinced through the gospel of your sinful condition, you judge yourself guilty, confess then what you are, and agree with GOD of your need of a Savior. You then accept GOD'S gift of His Only Begotten SON, the LAMB of GOD who "cleanses us from all unrighteousness" [1 Jn. 1:9], claiming Him LORD, [Rom. 10:9-10] "That if thou shalt confess with thy mouth the Lord Jesus, and shalt believe in thine heart that God hath raised him from the dead, thou shalt be saved. For with the heart man believeth unto righteousness; and with the mouth confession is made unto salvation".

I wanted to place my mother's unshakable confession of faith here because it's so personal, so powerful and moving I just wanted to share it, with the hopes it move you to be steadfast in your faith, in your pursuit to CHRIST-likeness and remain focused on the heavenly goal.

Mother's confession of faith:

I believe in God, The Father Almighty, The Maker of heaven and earth and Jesus Christ His Son our Lord, was conceived by the Holy Ghost, born by the virgin Mary, suffered under Pontus Pilate, crucified, died and buried the third day. He rose from the dead, descended to hell (He went to wake up Abraham, Isaac, Jacob and Joseph. They knew He was coming but died before Jesus came). Then He ascended into heaven and sat down by God the Father who will judge the living and the dead. I believe in The Holy Ghost, the Holy Baptist church, the forgiveness of sins, the resurrection of the body and life everlasting. Amen.

Now, since you followed GOD'S's pattern for salvation, your salvation is now sure and your sin debt settled. Now you must prepare your heart to receive GOD'S Word and the filling of The HOLY SPIRIT, the mind is the governing agent of the body, it is translated into the word "heart" in the Bible.

Proverbs 23:7a - "For as he thinketh in his heart, so is he".

The apostle Peter instructs us as well.

1Peter 1:13a - "Wherefore gird up the loins of your mind".

"Gird up" carries the idea of putting out of the way anything that will hinder the free action of the mind; the apostle Paul says, we must "purge out" or "*ekkathairo*" meaning to cleanse thoroughly. He talks about leaven in [1 Cor. 5:7] and refers to the hidden, silent, mysterious action of sin. Then he talks about clearing away negative folks with ungodly language; in other words, you must thoroughly clean-up your mind of any contaminating and corrupting influences that will soothe the sin hidden in your mind that would force your body to react in word or deed.

The Hebrew writer says, [Heb. 9:14] "The blood of Jesus purges the conscience of dead works" therefore, "purge from these", you would be a vessel unto honor, sanctified and meet for the master's use and prepared unto every good work" [2 Tim. 2:21].

2 Corinthians 5:17 - "Therefore, if any man be in Christ, he is a new creature, old things are passed away: behold, all things are become new".

Chapter Three

WHAT NAME ARE YOU ANSWERING TO

2 Corinthians 5:7 - "Old things are passed away".

At your conversion, you weren't given a new body without flaws. You received new life but remained in the old body with all of its cravings for the things of the world, but they are <u>contained, controlled, and restricted</u>.

JESUS prayed to The FATHER [Jn. 17:15] "I pray not that thou shouldest take them out of the world, but that thou shouldest keep them from the evil". In other words, from Thomasology, JESUS was asking the FATHER to <u>shockproof</u> us against the craving of the old man and its habits that would wake us in the night and force us to chase a high we couldn't catch.

Being shockproof won't allow you to operate as you once did. It forces you to make renovations, because the foundation you must build, a life pleasing to God, should be built on a rock. However, you can only build to the specifications of the rock. JESUS said, [Matt. 16:24] "if any man will come after me, <u>let him deny himself</u>, and take up his cross, and follow me". We received power to stand against the desires of the flesh, the world and the devil, because our relationship with Christ had broken its grip. We can now say "<u>no</u>" to self and everything attached to it. Even though those fleshly desires are still there, they can't make demands on your life as a master. Paul writes, [Rom. 6:12] "Let not sin therefore reign in your mortal body, that ye should obey it in the lusts thereof".

This chapter wasn't planned, it's imputed because I felt the need to talk a little more about the importance of what name you answer to. To many of us, a name really doesn't carry that much weight. But in biblical times, a name carried great significance. Might I add, the <u>nickname</u> the world placed on you is more than a label, it speaks of your character and is the <u>portal</u> by which the evil spirit claims you as his, because that name attaches you to the world. Notice please, the words of our LORD JESUS in [Matt. 12:43-45], "When the unclean spirit is gone out of a man, he walketh through dry places, seeking rest, and findeth none. Then he saith, I will return into my house from whence I came out; and when he is come, he findeth it empty, swept, and garnished. Then goeth he, and taketh with himself seven other spirits more wicked than himself, and they enter in and dwell there: and the last state of that man is worse than the first. Even so shall it be also unto this wicked generation".

Let me first put it in laymen terms: when your conversion has taken place and the spirit of the old man (habit) has been expelled and you stop doing what you were doing; he goes looking for another body. Paul calls the body a house [2 Cor. 5:1] to dwell in but finds no vacancies. So the spirit decides to go back to the body/house he came out of. The spirit finds the person's life cleaned up but the person is currently attempting to live right without the presence/power of The HOLY SPIRIT, which is the strong man who protects the person's life. Because there is no strong man, The HOLY SPIRIT, to resist the influence of the (habit) the evil spirit overpowers the man by bringing seven spirits (habits he can't resist) worse than himself, making the man's life worse than before.

Let us shine further light on the text so you remain watchful. When the devil left JESUS [Matt. 4:11] he didn't go away, he just moved within watching and striking distance. When Moses was negotiating Israel's release from Egypt, Pharoah told Moses to go into the plains and to stay within watching distance. The danger in that is, the eye is to act as a portal. When Lot left Abraham, he pitched towards (to look at) Sodom and then Lot was living in Sodom.

Point to Ponder: what the eyes are attracted to draws you into its current of influence; therefore, keep looking to JESUS the Author and Finisher of our faith.

Pharoah next suggests that Moses take everyone [Ex. 10:24] but leave the livestock. In other words, leave something that would act as a portal so Israel and Egypt would always have a connection with each other. It is the item a person leaves at your house as a portal to smother you with unwanted phone calls and unannounced visits. So it is in your Christian life, the enemy wants to keep a connection with you so he can show up whenever he want to and he does it through your worldly name.

Let me see if I can shine more light with the help of The HOLY SPIRIT. I was teaching Sunday school when a brother walked in that was under spiritual attack. He had lost everything, but Satan was after his soul. A few days before class, he ran into an old friend that was a running buddy from the streets. Upon their meeting, the young man addressed him with his nickname. Once we left the young man and were on our way, I had a natural desire to want to discuss with him the words that were in my mind, but the time was unseasoned and the HOLY SPIRIT muzzled me.   Now, as he walked into class I asked him, "How did it make you feel being called by your nickname"?

He said, "It didn't bother me".

I responded, "How is it, you being a child of GOD that you are comfortable being labeled by your past and not your present? How does that not bother you? You never wondered what you were putting on display? You never wondered! What did your old friend see, that he felt comfortable addressing the old man of flesh and not the new man in CHRIST? It would bother me!"

I'm trying to live a life pleasing to GOD and I'm displaying the person GOD saved me from instead of the person I used to be.   I want to represent Him on earth! Paul's closing words to the Thessalonians was [1 Thess. 5:21b-22] "hold fast to that which is good. Abstain from all appearance of evil". If it doesn't bother you to be called by your worldly name, it might be you haven't started walking in your new character yet.

Jacob is a prime example, he was given a new name Israel, prince with GOD [Gen. 32], yet in [Gen. 33:1] Jacob lifted up his eyes which signifies him walking by sight (the old man) and not by faith (the new man).

Point to ponder: The portal (sin habit) you leave open is the stumbling block that trips you up in your Christian walk for GOD. It is the portal that makes sin assessable, keeps you defending a life you have been liberated from, keeps you with a bad attitude by refusing to lift holy hands or sitting in church stagnated, keeps you sad, broken and running back to what's familiar in times of trouble.

My conversation with this brother affected another brother in my class by the name of George. One Tuesday night, George came to Bible Study and reported, "I want to say to all my Bethlehem brothers and sisters, don't call me George anymore. That is not my real name. That name was given me while I was in the streets. My real name is Nathaniel."

That's interesting! George in Greek means "tiller of the ground" and speaks of his worldly fleshly character. Nathaniel means "gift of God" and speaks of his godly character. What Nathaniel was doing was putting George to death, his worldly fleshly character, and embracing his new godly character by claiming his God given name Nathaniel.

Point to Ponder: Are you claiming the eternal blessings GOD has promised through your new name? Or, are you hanging on to false promises of your old name?

Your past ought to be your past. You can't live your past in your present. You can't live a life pleasing to GOD with the portal of your past open. There are two words in the book of Isaiah that carry a great deal of weight that most Christians never think about - [Isa. 43:1] "but now". You ought to be living in your "but now" [Isa. 43:1a]. By saying that, let me remind you that your conversion is made sure in an imperfect body with all of its desires under constraint, but that doesn't mean you won't have struggles in your Christian walk.

As the people of GOD, the nation of Israel, struggled with their faithfulness to GOD according to [Isa. 42], they were sinning constantly and refusing to turn back to the LORD, GOD did not respond to them with judgment. He did it out of love [Ps. 103:13] "Like a father pitieth his children, so the Lord pitieth them that fear him". GOD reached out to Israel in mercy and claimed them as His own [Isa. 43:1]. GOD said, "I created you, formed you, redeemed you, I called you by thy name; you art mine" live your "<u>but now</u>" and not your "<u>but then</u>". You do this by burying everything that connected you to the world. That is what Jacob did [Gen. 35:4]. He buried everything which connected his household to the world. You must get completely out of sight of that thing and that thing must be completely out of sight of you. When you're walking for GOD, you don't need to broadcast it. They will see it.

Acts 4:13 - "Now when they saw the boldness of Peter and John, and perceived that they were unlearned and ignorant men, they marvelled; and they took knowledge of them, that they had been with Jesus".

Before old friends see you, check your B's.
1) Be aware of what you're putting on display.
2) Be conscience of what they are calling you, and
3) Be aware of what you're answering to.

If your worldly friends are not uncomfortable with you in their midst or respect your new life in CHRIST, check what you are putting on display. If your godly presence don't affect their drinking, cursing, lying while you're in their company, don't be offended; just know your Christian character still needs some work. The work you need can't be found in the present company you are keeping. You need friends that will help sharpen you for Christ.

Point to Ponder: Digging in dirt will dull a tool. Taking fire in your bosom will burn clothes. Walking on hot coals will burn feet. Hanging around ungodly people with no desire for GOD will sooner or later convince you to return to your old ways of life. Change your scenery and change your friends.

Now that you followed GOD's divine pattern for salvation, cleared your heart, checked what you focus on, and closed the portal so there is no connection with the world, you are now conscience of what you put on display and the people you are in fellowship with. Now what?

2 Corinthians 6:17 - "Wherefore come out from among them, and be ye separate, saith the Lord, and touch not the unclean thing; and I will receive you".

Isaiah 43:1 – "But now thus saith the Lord that created thee, O Jacob, and he that formed thee, O Israel, Fear not: for I have redeemed thee, I have called thee by thy name; thou art mine".

Chapter Four

NOW WHAT DO I DO?

Genesis 17:1 - "I am the Almighty God; walk before me, and be thou perfect".

There are two words in the scripture above that must be understood, "walk" and "perfect". The word "walk" speaks more than "walk about", but can also mean a life or a lifestyle which includes thoughts, words and deeds. The word "perfect" or *"teleious"* in Greek, is not sinless but points to an aim or purpose. It is the point of reaching full development or maturity of godliness. The apostle Paul writes:

Ephesians 4:13 - "Till we all come in the unity of the faith, and of the knowledge of the Son of God, unto a perfect man, unto the measure of the stature of the fullness of Christ".

Now that you are a child of GOD, the servant of the Most High, the basic problem you are probably facing is the question, "Now what do I do?" This is the point where you can become invisible in plain sight, in other words, a religious wreck. This is where you begin to develop into the strong servant for GOD that the Lord desires you to be.

When I was accepted in the royal family of GOD, I had an unexplainable hunger to know the Lord. I asked questions and received very few answers. Here is the grave mistake that I made and the lesson I learned. Don't be spiritually ignorant by joining a church without consulting The LORD GOD Almighty for directions. No one can satisfy your spiritual hunger, regardless of whether they call themselves a minister or have another title or label. Be careful, because all are not carrying the life sustaining bread.

JESUS said [Matt. 22:14] "For many are called but few are chosen". John instructs us on what to do concerning those people operating under false pretense.

2 John 9-10 - "whosoever transgresseth, and abideth not in the doctrine of Christ, hath not God. He that abideth in the doctrine of Christ, he hath both the Father and the Son. If there come any unto you, and bring not this doctrine, receive him not into your house, neither bid him God speed".

Amaziah was priest doing the time of Amos [Amos 7], but he had nothing to say about GOD. So it is today. Many fill the pulpit and teach from the Bible without heaven's approval. I was out of place after conversion and didn't know it, because I never asked GOD for direction. Soon, the result became evident. I asked my pastor a question that I was struggling with in the Word of GOD. I saw in his eyes that he, too, struggled to find an answer. He said to me, "I got mine you got to get yours". (Pause a minute) What?? I was very disappointed and sad; I felt confused and at a loss. I don't believe he knew the depth of damage he caused within me that day. What do you do when the person who claims to be an ambassador of CHRIST closes the door on your seeking growth and development in the LORD?

Point to Ponder: If you find yourself spiritually sad and depressed and the excitement of being a Christian is "going...going...GONE" because some out of season Christian has disappointed you, then you need to know that the HOLY SPIRIT gives direction for a spiritual uplifting.

Don't give up! Don't give in to the voice that's saying, "They are all the same!" You need to know all is **not** all the same. There are still some true servants who have not bowed their knees to Baal.

1Kings 19:18 - "Yet I have left me seven thousand in Israel, all the knees which have not bowed unto Baal, and every mouth which hath not kissed him".

Take a moment to talk to GOD about your situation and your desire to know Him (He knows your heart). It's not too early or too late to ask GOD for direction. Sometimes the Spirit speaks to us and sometimes He speak through people to us; sometimes the SPIRIT comes, and sometimes He sends other people to us [Acts 8:26-27], so was my experience.

The HOLY SPIRIT sent my brother, Cleveland, to me to direct me to a spiritual uplifting recovery and to bring me instructions to re-ignite The HOLY GHOST fire in me again. He said, "Lou, if you get under Rev. L. Jackson (now deceased), he can help you. He is a "Bible teacher".

I inquired of the LORD GOD, "Should I go and I received a strong urge to be in his presence?"

When I sought out Pastor Jackson, he didn't have a mega-church; he had only a small congregation, but he was on fire for GOD. When he spoke, he brought the Word of GOD and it became alive in me. I attached myself to him because I wanted what he had and what he put on display was priceless. That was the imprint the prophet Elijah made on Elisha when he took his mantle and wrapped it together and smote the Jordan and the waters divided and the two crossed on dry land.

2 Kings 2:8-9 - "that Elijah said unto Elisha, Ask what I shall do for thee, before I be taken away from thee. And Elisha said, I pray thee, let a double portion of thy spirit be upon me".

That is what your spiritual instructor should do. They should inspire you to want more - more of the SPIRIT, more of JESUS, more power, more of GOD'S Word, more of His grace and mercy. Then he/she should motivate you to DO more. Notice the words JESUS said to His disciples:

John 14:12 - "the works that I do shall he do also; and greater works than these shall he do; because I go unto my Father".

Notice JESUS is not biased or jealous. There is none of the "I got mine and you got to get yours" mentality. JESUS expected His disciples to do more and reach more. As a child of GOD, this power is available for you as well, if you would only ask. JESUS said [Matt. 7:7] "Ask, and it shall be given you, seek, and ye shall find; knock, and it shall be opened unto you". James gives a note of caution [Jas. 1:6a] "But let him ask in faith, nothing wavering". In other words, don't ask with an ulterior motive or hidden agenda for personal gain.

Saul asked, "What will thou have me to do?" Jesus says to Saul [Acts 9:6], "Arise, go into the city, and it shall be told thee what thou must do." The HOLY SPIRIT guides us to the servant of GOD that will instruct us in the things pertaining to the LORD. To ignore the HOLY SPIRIT's direction and bypass the servant of GOD is to wander in the wilderness of this world.

Let me run in the woods a minute and give you an idea of what I'm talking about. I took my daughter, Ophelia, to San Antonio, Texas to explore a cave there. Her question to me was, "Dad, are they going to put us in a cave and we have to find our way out?"

"No, Sweets," I replied, "it doesn't work that way. They will give us an experienced guide who will lead us through the cave safely."

Upon our arrival, we all were gathered in this large area where the signs along the walls were warning signs of things we couldn't carry with us on the journey. There were also signs warning not to venture out alone because of pending dangers. We were instructed to wait for the tour guide and follow all of his/her instructions. That's exactly what JESUS commanded His disciples in [Acts 1:4-5], that they should not depart from Jerusalem, but wait for the promise of the FATHER. "For John truly baptized with water; but ye shall be baptized with the Holy Ghost not many days hence". The HOLY SPIRIT will lead and guide you through all truths [Jn. 16:13] "Howbeit when he, the Spirit of truth, is come, he will guide you into all truth: for he shall not speak of himself; but whatsoever he shall hear, that shall he speak: and he will show you things to come".

Regardless of what you think you know, lay it aside and rest assured the guide/HOLY SPIRIT knows the way [Josh. 3:4b] "that ye may know the way by which ye must go: for ye have not passed this way heretofore". On this Christian journey, there are some things that will hinder your walking for GOD and they must be stripped off [Heb. 12:1] "every weight"; [Eph. 4:22] "the former conversation the old man"; and all these of [Col. 3:8] "anger, wrath, malice, blasphemy, filthy communication out of your mouth".

When The LORD JESUS CHRIST met Saul of Tarsus on the Damascus road the LORD struck him with blindness, blinded him to the things of the world and anything within himself that would exalt itself above God [1 Jn. 2:16] "For all that is in the world, the lust of the flesh, and the lust of the eyes, and the pride of life, is not of the Father, but is of the world". The LORD blinded Saul to a religion and introduced him to His personhood [Acts 9:5] "I am Jesus whom thou persecuting" and then turned him over to his spiritual guide Ananias. Notice how Saul is to know his spiritual guide. GOD gave him a vision of one Ananias [Vs.12] "coming in putting his hand on him, that he might receive his sight". Where your spiritual sight is enlightened and the uplifting of your spirit is ignited is the place GOD ordained for your spiritual growth.

Here is the monkey wrench that can cause you to go many years sitting in church undeveloped. Maybe you feel the strong pull of The Holy Spirit on your life directing you to GOD'S servant, but you hadn't made any effort because you would have to make changes (maybe leaving the family church or getting under someone family and friends don't like because he/she steps on their sinful toes) or you would have to give up some position that make you look like the church big shot. Abraham didn't receive GOD'S full blessings where he was. Notice GOD'S words to him:

Genesis 12:1-2a - "Now the Lord had said unto Abram, Get thee out of thy country, and from thy kindred, and from thy father's house, unto a land that I will shew thee: and I will make of thee a great nation, and I will bless thee".

In order to get something from God, you must be willing to give up something for GOD. JESUS said to his disciples [Matt. 16:24] "If any man will come after me, let him deny himself, and take up his cross, and follow me". [1 Sam. 15:22b] "Behold, to obey is better than sacrifice".

Point to Ponder: What is more important, the satisfaction of the body or the salvation and growth of the soul?

Notice the words of our LORD JESUS [Mk. 8:35] "For whosoever will save his life shall lose it; but whosoever shall lose his life for my sake and the gospel's, the same shall save it". Are you where GOD placed you or are you where it's comfortable? Being comfortable in your Christianity is another way of saying, "I'm conformed in religion". Being conformed means you are just going along, to get along. The apostle

Paul says [Rom. 12:2] "be ye transformed" (be different), think different, act different, live different; that's what JESUS was instructing his listening audience as He taught His famous sermon on the mount [Matt. 5:44] "love your enemies, bless them that curse you, do good to them that hate you, and pray for them which despitefully use you, and persecute you". Be different, salt of the earth different, light of the world different, turning the other cheek different, going two miles different, and forgiving and loving enemies different. Being different makes enemies not friends. Being different brings uncomfortable conditions such as unkind words from the church deadbeats (those who have special seats and attend every church function but are still under-developed and have a problem with <u>your</u> growth). GOD places us in hostile places to teach us to trust Him, even among enemies who teach us. He can protect us, regardless how they disfigure their faces [Jer.1:8]. GOD says, "I am with you, I got you."

In [1 Kgs.17:5] GOD sends the prophet Elijah to the brook Cherith, an uncomfortable isolated place with an intermixture of hills and valleys covered with dense woods, and supplied his needs with fresh water in the brook and unclean birds delivering bread and meat twice a day. John the Baptist wasn't in the king's court [Lk. 7:24], but in the wilderness, eating locust and wild honey. Look what the apostle John says about Jesus [Jn. 1:3] "All things were made by him; and without him was not anything made that was made", but we hear JESUS talking about the condition he was in [Matt. 8:20] "The foxes have holes, and the birds of the air have nests; but the Son of man hath not where to lay his head".

The place GOD sends you to may not be comfortable, but it will be productive. Comfortable places in religion are really wilderness places for a church member who enjoys going in circles and making rules as they go. It's the place where the churches undeveloped members are formed. Seasoned, long-term church members who never attended Bible study or Sunday school, never felt the power of the HOLY SPIRIT, and never led anyone to CHRIST; they just sit comfortable in a religion because nobody ever challenged them to spiritually engage.

Here is a two-question test you can perform to determine if you're in the right place for spiritual growth:
    1) Did you choose the place or did the HOLY SPIRIT lead you there, and;

2) Is the same SPIRIT unveiling the mystery of the gospel of JESUS CHRIST in preaching and teaching?

If so, then the gospel ought to create a hunger in your innermost being to know the LORD, your spiritual sight should be recovered, and a heart after GOD will be developed. The spiritual leader GOD, through The HOLY SPIRIT, has placed you under authority which ought to, when he speaks about The LORD that you love so much, bring out a spiritual hunger in you that you need to have more.

Are you hungry yet?

Colossians 3:16 - "Let the word of Christ dwell in you richly in all wisdom; teaching and admonishing one another in psalms and hymns and spiritual songs, singing with grace in your hearts to the Lord".

Chapter Five

<u>ARE YOU HUNGRY YET?</u>

1 Peter 2:2 - "As newborn babes, desire the sincere milk of the word, that ye may grow thereby".

I would like to drop a nugget of mother's wisdom here. I found myself back home living with my mom, my job kept me on the road days at a time, and when I made it home, mom would always say, "Lou, go ahead get your bath and when you get out I will have your dinner on the table".

But this one particular evening when I came in from work I was met with a question, "Lou, are you ready to eat"?

I said, No ma'am, I'm not hungry".

Her response was, "<u>You don't eat because you are hungry; you eat to keep from getting hungry</u>"!

With this concept I would like to enter this part of the book to awaken your spiritual senses to the mistakes we make and continue to make unaware. If you attend church regularly or part time and sit in the pew listening (a little more light would be shined on this later) you are asleep and need a divine awakening. You need a touch of The HOLY SPIRIT to awaken your mind/your inner man to rise up and hear the word of the LORD.

In [1 Kgs. 19:5], "Elijah is asleep under a juniper tree and an angel touches him and says to him, "Arise and eat". It is vital that you do. Food is the product the body consumes to produce energy; the energy is the fuel we burn when putting forth effort in accomplishing a task. The Word of GOD is the product the spiritual man needs to empower him to accomplish the will of GOD and to fulfill the purpose GOD has planned for your life. When Elijah ate he, according to [1 Kgs. 19:8], "went in the strength of that meat forty days and forty nights".

Point to Ponder: How often have you neglected eating God's Word because you didn't feel hungry? Just add up how many Bible study and Sunday school classes you missed, and how many times outside of church you neglected the need to read God's Word since you've been saved, and you have your answer.

Let me put something else on your mind in the form of a question that only you can answer. For the duration of the time you claim to be a child of GOD, did it ever bother you that you never suffered "hunger pains"? It never crossed your mind, that in order to abide in CHRIST is to abide in His Word with promise?

John -15:7 - "If ye abide in me, and my words abide in you, ye shall ask what ye will, and it shall be done unto you".

More overly, we go through a developmental stage as we move from milk to meat. Many who wear the label "Christians" have deceived themselves to believe they're born fully grown and never need to go through a developmental process. However, everything that experiences a birth grows; and everything that grows, produces something! A seed grows into a plant, and produces fruit; an egg grows into a chick and produces a reproduction cycle; and, a sperm grows into a person and produces works. If everything born grows into something, why are people who claim to be a Christian caught up in this pseudo-misconception that he/she is exempt from spiritual development?

What do you think would happen if you completely refuse to eat? Would you not eventually suffer malnutrition and die? How much more do you think you can live minus the life sustaining bread of life? Jesus said, [Jn. 6:35] "I am the bread of life: he that cometh to me shall never hunger; and he that believeth on me shall never thirst". In the gospel of John [Jn. 1], JESUS is identified as The Word, "*logos*", living Word [Vs.1], and in Him is life [Vs.4], then in [Jn. 6:63] Jesus said, "the words that I speak unto you they are Spirit and they are life" and still in [Jn. 6:55-56] "For my flesh is meat indeed, and my blood is drink indeed. He that eateth my flesh, and drinketh my blood, dwelleth in me, and I in him".

When you refuse to feast on the Word of GOD, you are refusing the very life of GOD and the fellowship GOD ushered in through His Son the "*logos*". Too many believe they've been given a free pass when the preacher told them simply, "Find your place, get in your place, and stay in your place."

Newborn babies are incapable of finding their place on their own. As a matter of fact, GOD never intended for you to find your own place. GOD knew that as a newborn babe, you would need someone to instruct and guide you. Jesus promised the disciples in [Jn. 16:7] "When I leave I will send the HOLY SPIRIT and He will guide you". When Philip was directed to join himself to the man of Ethiopia [Acts 8], who was reading the prophet Isaiah, he asked, "Do you understand what you are reading?" His response was, "How can I except some man should guide me".

Every job I worked on, the supervisor didn't tell me, "Find your place, get in your place, and stay in your place." No, he gave me someone knowledgeable of the job to train me about the position I was to fill. When I joined church, I wasn't given any literature on what was expected of me as a child of GOD; I wasn't given a dress code. Nobody told me the importance of reading GOD'S Word, the right way to worship GOD, or how to pray and have my prayers answered. I was clueless. Sure, the pastor gave me a Bible when I asked for one, but he didn't teach me how to study it; he didn't point out specific scriptures I needed to digest as a new born babe in CHRIST.

Let me put a pin right here and run in the woods a minute. There are two kinds of mothers; one I call a production mother and the other a nursing mother. The production mother only has babies without any desire for its care and well-being; she's simple minded like the ostrich, which lays her eggs in the dust to keep them warm [Job 37:14-15], and then forgets she or other animals can break them as they trample around. But the nursing mother cares and nurtures her newborn; she protects, instructs and feeds.

Point to Ponder: There are two kinds of ministers; the hireling and the man GOD appoints. The hireling is only concerned for himself and can care less for the babe in CHRIST. The man GOD appoints wants the best for the people of GOD; he feeds and nourishes them with knowledge and understanding and protects them to the point of risking his own life.

When you are truly born again, you're born with an overwhelming desire to know The Lord and that desire is fulfilled in studying the Word of GOD. Every newborn baby is born with a tremendous appetite. They will receive whatever you put in their mouth. But for newborn babes, not everything is good. Meat, for example, will choke a newborn. As newborn babes in CHRIST, there are two things we must be concerned with:
1) What you eat and
2) Who you eat from

GOD alone gives this job to His ministers, not a seminary or any man, GOD alone.

Jeremiah 3:15 - "And I will give you pastors according to mine heart, which shall feed you with knowledge and understanding".

He will appoint one who has the mind of God towards GOD's people. One who will teach the mind of GOD through the Word of GOD by aide of The HOLY SPIRIT, unveiling the deep secrets hidden from the wise and prudent in the Word of GOD. Are you hungry yet or are you eating to keep from getting hungry? There are too many undernourished Christians because they didn't feel hungry and so they missed the meals served in Sunday school or Bible study. Remember, you don't eat because you're hungry, but to keep from getting hungry.

A wise mother would feed her baby formulated milk. The apostle Peter says the spiritual formula for a babe in CHRIST [1 Pet. 2:2] is to "desire the sincere milk of the word". Notice, he commands the newborn Christian to "desire", "*epipotheo*", meaning an intense craving. Another time the word "*epipotheo*" is used, Paul used it in the context in [Phil. 2:26] where it's translated in the text where Paul talked about sending his companion and fellow worker back to Philippi because he was homesick. Homesickness would make you whine and look sickly. That was the appearance of Nehemiah in [Neh. 2:26], as he performed his duties before the king, the king asked him why are you long-faced seeing you're not sick? In short Nehemiah says, "I'm homesick"!

Let me run in the woods a minute to shine a personal light on this subject. My first time traveling to Atlanta, GA, everything went well during the day; but when night set in I became restless and couldn't sleep. I wanted to go home. I started whining, "I wanna go home!" I was so homesick, so I started packing. My friend said, "Do you know how far New Orleans is from here"?

My response was a snapping, "I don't care! I'll walk home!"

That's the kind of craving Peter says you ought to have for the Word of GOD. That craving ought to be so strong, so intense, that nothing can stop you from getting it. Your inability to read won't keep you from Bible study or Sunday school; neither will you settle for anything less, like the spiritual junk foods, the today's minister sling across the pulpit on Sunday, the sloppy joe sermons with no JESUS, the sweet water prosperity messages that sends a false fulfilled satisfaction geared for the flesh that never produce spiritual growth.

Here is another example. I came up in a poor family; my mother struggled to put food on the table. One evening my baby sister was crying uncontrollably and my mother said to me, "Lou, go and fill the baby bottle with water up to here and put a half teaspoon of sugar in it and bring it here."

I did as she asked and without question. She shook the bottle to mix the water and sugar and gave it to my baby sister and the crying ceased. What she did was trick the baby's brain to believe it was receiving the food it needed. That is what the sermons with no JESUS does. It tricks the newborn brain to believe that it received what it needed until the test comes and you fail to stand and withstand. It's important that you remember GOD's Word is vital to your spiritual growth. If you're not receiving it, then it's certain you will suffer spiritual malnutrition and you would have no strength to finish the journey.

In [1Kgs. 19] we find the prophet Elijah under a juniper tree, fast asleep after leading a successful campaign upon Mount Carmel. An angel wakes him and encourages him to eat for he says, "The journey is too great for thee". That is why Paul encouraged the sailors who were trying to navigate a ship in a storm [Acts 27:34] "take some meat: for this is for your health". You can't be strong in the LORD without feasting on the Word of GOD; and you won't feast without a desire. Notice the "craving" should be after the "sincere milk" the word "sincere" or *"adolos"* has a meaning unadulterated. It carries the idea of being unmixed with anything else.

When my eldest child was born, Similac came in two different formulas. One was ready mix - just pour straight from the can into the baby bottle and the other you mix with water. The one you add water to, you get more but it breaks down the nutrition the baby needed. The first kind wasn't diluted and everything the baby needed for development he/she received. So, Peter's warning is: "Don't mix GOD's Word with your own opinion or imagination; don't mix it with education or religion, philosophy or pleasures, fortune or fame. It will nullify GOD's Word making it of no effect."

Everything for your spiritual growth and development is contained straight within the Holy Bible. GOD says, [Deut. 4:2] "ye shall not add unto the word which I command you, neither shall ye diminish ought from it, that ye may keep the commandments of the Lord your God which I command you". Contained within the unadulterated Word of GOD are ingredients that produce faith, hope, joy, peace and empowerment for the inner man.

Paul writes, [Rom. 10:17] "So then faith cometh by hearing, and hearing by the word of God". Notice, he didn't say faith comes by listening, but <u>hearing</u>. There is a difference between listening and hearing. In listening, words may never penetrate/resonate the mind, but hearing means being attentive, absorbing what being said, and making applications to one's life for the betterment. May I say, gaining faith may or may not be difficult, but the trying of your faith will ruffle your spiritual feathers while the storm/hardship/difficult situation prove your faith genuine as it develops within you <u>patience</u> [Jas. 1:3].

Patience proves itself to be important in difficult situations. It's the virtue that helps you endure hardships as a good soldier [2 Tim. 2:3]. It gives you the endurance to wait on the LORD by not timetabling GOD's response to you but faithfully waiting no matter how long it takes. Remember the words of Isaiah [Isa. 40:31a], "But they that wait upon the Lord shall renew their strength". When you give out all in the service of GOD, doing that which GOD commands expect a renewing of strength.

Gauge Yourself

When my children were younger, I had a "gauge your growth" day. I remembered how proud my kids were to know they had grown, so much so they began a contest amongst themselves to see who can outgrow the other. I tell each member in my Bible class, "Gauge your spiritual growth". If there's an area in your Christianity that you need to work on, write it down and ask GOD to help you work on it. You have a problem with forgiving people? Write it down and ask GOD to help you work on it.

When is the last time you measured your spiritual growth? How much have you grown since claiming CHRIST as your SAVIOR? Are you claiming to be what you haven't grown into? Are little things still getting the best of your emotions, feelings still being wounded over stuff you know shouldn't upset you? Are you able now to forgive because you can see the real enemy behind the act or action? When you gauge yourself, be honest with yourself, and remember you need GOD's help to reach the goal of Christ-likeness.

Something else I tell my Bible study class, if you gauge yourself and don't see any growth after putting in the work, then find a place where you can grow. It's about you growing in Christ, not Thomas. Your growth becomes visible when things happen that would have triggered the old man, but now the new man in Christ is engaged.

The Measuring Rod

Jesus is the measuring rod and your growth is being marked off by you becoming Christ-like. Are you seeing flashes of the LORD in your attitude towards others? Are you dealing with life situations differently? How tall are you, are you measuring up to the WORD of GOD? Are you responding to people with patience? Are you treating others the way you want them to treat you? Can you forgive and forget, remembering the great debt you couldn't pay GOD and He forgave you and casted the i.o.u in the sea of forgetfulness, never to bring it up again or hold a grudge against you for it? Before you react to negativity, are you asking what would JESUS do, and waiting on Him to direct your course of action?

Remember, the enemy wants you to omit GOD from the decision making. You can't act without including the LORD. It is He that has a plan for your life and it is He who will direct you to the proper course of action you must take that your godly integrity is upheld and He receives glory to His Name.

Are you hungry yet? Remember, you don't eat because you are hungry; you eat to keep from getting hungry.

2 Timothy 3:16-17 – "All scripture is given by inspiration of God, and is profitable for doctrine, for reproof, for correction, for instruction in righteousness: That the man of God may be perfect, thoroughly furnished unto all good works".

Chapter Six

WHAT IS REQUIRED?

John 12:26a - "If any man serve me, let him follow me".

Many of us live our lives up to a point. We set limitations, boundaries, and points we will not go beyond before we say, "That's enough"! In relationships, you could do or say this or this, but definitely not that. For the moment you do or say THAT, your relationship dissolves. In religion, people would be regular church attendants as long as you talk about prosperity or being blessed. But start talking about sin in Bible study or Sunday school and start discussing the things God has a problem with that matches their secret lifestyle and you have people who stop attending your church.

There's an analogy of this very thing in [Jn. 6:66-68]. JESUS had many followers, but He said something that offended them. Because of that, they began to abandon Him because they had reached the threshold they refused to cross. As JESUS watched them leave, He turned to the ones who had been with Him and asked, *"Will ye also go away"*? Peter's response was, "To whom could we go, who can give us what you give, *thou hast the words of eternal life*". From this point, Jesus is moving towards Jerusalem to fulfill His mission without the disciples fully understanding what that mission consisted of.

In [Vs.20], our text opens by talking about certain Greeks who became members of the fellowship. They had a desire to see JESUS, which points to the first-fruits of a great Gentile harvest that will result from His death. It's at this junction of JESUS ministry that He announces that the climax of his mission had arrived and he was about to lay down his life.

Many have claimed to be followers of CHRIST without fully understanding what *requirements* are attached to such a claim, so JESUS lays out what is required to be a follower and serve. In our printed text, He says, "I*f any man serve me, let him follow me*". It seems like a simple requirement, but this simple requirement carries with it the difficulty of conduct. If you notice the conjunction "*if*", it's a conditional particle in the Greek. The word "*if*" it sits right in the middle of the word "*life*". JESUS dealt with the condition of the mind pertaining to life in [Vs.25]. He says, "He that loveth his life shall lose it; and he that hateth his life in this world shall keep it unto life eternal". He's warning about selfishness - being excessively concerned for one's self, one's own advantage, pleasure or welfare regardless of who you have to hurt to get your way.

A selfish person doesn't like changes. They are the ones who claim to be Christians but still have ego trips. They continue hanging out in clubs and at parties, practicing social drinking, chasing the wind, and living in false dreams in casinos. They toss Mardi Gras beads off floats, bet on ball games, and gossip with all the knowledge and human wisdom and participate in anything of the world that excites their emotions. These individuals are half-hearted servants.

In [Matt. 6:24] Jesus lays out the difficulty that would hinder one from being a faithful servant of GOD and then lays GOD and the world side by side and says to us "Y*e cannot serve both*" so choose one. That's what Elijah told those Baal worshippers upon Mount Carmel. [1 Kgs. 18:21] "If the Lord be God, follow him: but if Baal, then follow him. And the people answered him not a word", because they were caught up in a religion called selfishness. Selfishness will stop dedicated service in its tracks because James says [Jas. 1:8] "A double minded man is unstable in all of his ways". JESUS, the Revelator, didn't tell us [Rev.

3:15] to be *"**cold and hot**"*, but make a choice and be cold <u>or</u> hot.

Once you settle the temporal from the eternal, the truth from the false, and *"choose this day the God you will serve"* and if that GOD is The LORD GOD ALMIGHTY, then JESUS invites you to service. Come again to "and he that hateth his life in this world shall keep it unto life eternal". First of all you become a judge before you become a servant. You see life's true value without The LORD in it and you hate it. The Greek word *"miseo"* meaning to "detest" states that whatever you detest you detach yourself from, and being convinced by the gospel.

JESUS is the CHRIST and The HOLY SPIRIT applying the blood of JESUS to the conscience convicting you so you commit yourself to CHRIST. Notice the text please, [Vs.26a] "If any man serve me, let him follow me". Notice the word "**follow**" from the Greek word "a*koloutheō*" meaning <u>*to be in the same way with; to accompany*</u>. Amos posed a good question. [Am. 3:3] "Can two walk together, except they be agreed"? He's talking about continual companionship. You can't walk together with The LORD in fellowship until you meet, talk, and agree. This was the experience of Saul of Tarsus in [Acts 9] when he met JESUS on the way, and communed and submitted himself unto the LORD. Notice again the word **"follow"**. It's a twofold action - it's positive and negative and it carries the idea of being separated from something in order to be separated unto something else.

To follow the LORD JESUS, you must separate yourself from worldly people. [2 Cor. 6:17] "Wherefore come out from among them, and be separate"; you must separate yourself from worldly practices [Matt. 23:3] "but do not after their works: for they say, and do not"; and then, you must separate yourself from philosophies [Col. 2:8] *"Beware lest any man spoil you through philosophy and vain deceit, after the tradition of men, after the rudiments of the world, and not after Christ"*.

Then to **"follow"**, you must be submissive (the action or fact of accepting or yielding to a superior force or to the will or authority of another person). In the text, JESUS submitted to the will of the FATHER in order that He might glorify His name. To be submissive to CHRIST is to imitate Him now in humility and later in honor [Rom. 8:17; 2 Tim. 2:12a]. The way to glory is through death to self and through service to GOD and man. I need you to notice one more thing about the word "**follow**". It is in the present tense which mean *continuation or persistency*. It gives the idea of faithfulness.

Faithfulness is obedience without excuses. Faithfulness is doing without questions. Faithfulness is standing when the conditions are not favorable. Faithfulness is getting out the boat at Jesus' command in the middle of a storm. Faithfulness is standing up for Christ in the face of an angry crowd. Faithfulness is standing on right when wrong is persistent for attention. Faithfulness is going, even if the outcome results in injury or death.

Paul says, [1 Cor. 4:2] *"Moreover it is required in stewards, that a man be found faithful."* Faithfulness has nothing to do with selfishness. As a matter a fact, faithfulness goes against everything selfishness stands for. The apostle John writes [Rev. 2:10] *"be thou faithful unto death"*. Not until somebody hurts your feelings, rolls their eyes or stands in opposition to you, but be faithful in spite of their faces or ill treatment and receive your reward.

Revelation 2:10b - "And I will give thee a crown of life".

Chapter Seven

<u>BE LIKE A TREE</u>

Psalm 1:3a – "And he shall be like a tree planted by the rivers of water".

Many times JESUS spoke in parables. He took an earthly story His listeners were familiar with and applied a heavenly meaning since we can't utter or understand heaven's language. David used the imagery of a tree to describe what a flourishing Christian life really looks like. "Like a tree planted" the word "planted" or *"shaw-thol"* means to transplant. In other words, the tree was somewhere else and brought to the river's edge.

GOD made man and planted him in the Garden of Eden. When man sinned, GOD dispelled him. While the nation of Israel was in Egypt, they didn't bring glory to GOD's name, but GOD heard their cries. He sent justice to Egypt to uproot the tree (Israel) and brought the tree (Israel) from the powers of a great enemy, carried them through an impossible Red Sea, protected them from the difficulties of heathen nations and the hardships of the wilderness, and brought them into the land of promise.

Isaiah says [Isa. 5:1-2] GOD "planted it (the tree, Israel) on a fruitful hill" but it didn't produce good fruits. It only (according to the prophet) "brought forth wild grapes", so it became a tree taking up space. JESUS gives us an analogy of this in the parable of the barren fig tree.

Luke13:6-9 - "He spake also this parable; a certain man had a fig tree planted in his vineyard; and he came and sought fruit thereon, and found none. Then said he unto the dresser of his vineyard, Behold, these three years I come seeking fruit on this fig tree, and find none: cut it down; why cumbereth it the ground? And he answering said unto him, Lord, let it alone this year also, till I shall dig about it, and dung it: and if it bear fruit, well: and if not, then after that thou shalt cut it down".

Let's personalize it. The man is GOD, the tree is you planted in the world, and the dresser/gardener is the LORD JESUS who begs HIS FATHER to give HIM time to perform a work on you. Allow me to say it the way JESUS said it as HE hung between sky and earth. "FATHER forgive them they know not what they do". By HIS grace and mercy HE offers you salvation through the gospel and you gave a heartbroken response. GOD then plucked you up out of the muck and mire and transplanted you in HIS BELOVED SON [1 Jn. 5:20].

This is the position where you really need to be careful. The word "careful" really means "be alert". The words of our LORD are very helpful here, [Rev. 2:25] "But that which ye have already hold fast till I come". Are you aware of what you really have? You went through a process from sinner to saint, you were made alive and blessed with all spiritual blessings in heavenly places in CHRIST [Eph. 1:3], but there are actions going on around you that would prevent you from drawing on those spiritual resources and if you're not aware, it could reverse your position. There are three negatives in [Ps. 1:1] the blessed man avoids and two positives he must embrace to be liken to a tree that he may draw his resources.

First the negatives. You must refuse the path of that person/persons who has no fear of GOD before his/her face and you must not, notice the word "council" meaning advice; you must not ask or accept their advice to help you walk upright before GOD. Notice something else, you must avoid their principles, rules, and not be inspired by their drive for riches or fame. The reason is, you are different! Say it, "I'm different", moved and directed by the Word of GOD and not man's imagination; say it,

"I'm different", I was chosen by CHRIST and not voted in CHRIST by the world. "I'm different", walking by faith and not by sight, going against the pull of this world's system and trusting The LORD JESUS CHRIST the author and finisher of my faith.

Secondly, there's something else you must not do, you must not "stand in the way of sinners". Sinners are folks that would do just about anything and indulge in open sin. Standing in the way doesn't mean blocking the way of their having access to the LORD JESUS CHRIST, it means to stand with them, to agree with them in their ungodly lifestyle.

Paul advice to us in [1 Cor. 5:10-11] to not keep company with them. Solomon's strong warning is, [Pro. 4:14-15] "Enter not into the path of the wicked, and go not in the way of evil men. Avoid it, pass not by it, turn from it, and pass away". Once you accept the path they are on, you are conforming to their conduct and lifestyle. Paul's instruction is [Rom. 12:2] "And be not conformed but be transformed". Look at Peter when he denounced knowing JESUS. Later we find him in the courtyard with those who condemned his LORD. In [Mk. 14:67] "Peter warming himself", mean Peter had abandoned the path The LORD had called him to walk and he was keeping company, in fellowship with those who indulge in open sin, and was in agreement with those who condemned his LORD.

Point to Ponder: If you refuse the path you would never stand with the condemned.

When the devil tried to get JESUS to abandon the path GOD set before HIM, JESUS stood firm and rebuked the devil with the WORD of GOD, He said, "It is written." The writer of Hebrews states, [Heb. 12:2] "Looking unto Jesus the author and finisher of our faith; who for the joy that was set before him endured the cross, despising the shame, and is set down at the right hand of the throne of GOD". There's one more hurdle you must clear, you must not "sit in the seat of the scornful". That is loots meaning to mock; you're comfortable now doing what every condemned person is doing, mocking GOD and the people of GOD.

The scene is played out before our eyes in [Matt. 27:38-44]. Those who crucified CHRIST, the chief priests, scribes and elders, were joined by those who pass by, then those who were being crucified <u>with</u> CHRIST began to agree with the condemned and rail on the LORD [Vs.44]. But Luke says [Lk. 23:39-40], one of the two thieves rebuked the other and asked JESUS for forgiveness and went to paradise while the other to the torment chamber of hell. Again, be alert that you don't enter the path of the ungodly, agreeing with sinners and end up where you were saved from, mocking GOD and condemned to damnation.

Now notice please the two positives [Ps. 1:2], that liken us to a flourishing tree; the words I delight and meditate on are expressions of love. Let me give an analogy of what I'm talking about so the psalmist words could resonate in your heart.

If you ever received a love letter, like me, then you know how it makes you feel. The first love letter I received had me so overcome with emotion I could hardly stand. I tried to open the letter with care, but before I knew it I was ripping through the envelope trying to get to the content. My heart was pounding so hard I could hear it beating inside my chest. Finally, I reached the letter tucked neatly away inside the envelope. As I read the letter, I could hear her voice speaking the words as if she was there talking to me in person. When I finished reading the letter, I put it in my pocket and it stayed on my mind, the words she spoke. Every now and then, I pulled the letter out to read the places where she said, "I love you!"

So David says GOD's WORD is a love letter to His beloved, the *"ekklesia"*, <u>you</u>! As you read God's Word, you can hear Him speaking to your heart, romancing your (*kardia*) mind with expressions of His love; so much that you are constantly thinking about His Words day and night and you respond to His love letter through prayer. Because of your close connection with GOD, loving and meditating on His written Word, and responding to Him in constant prayer, the psalmist likens you to a tree.

The first identifiable trait in a tree, noticeably, is its strength. The apostle Paul says to us [Eph. 6:10] "Be strong in the LORD and in the power of His might". Feasting on the Word of GOD strengthens you to stand and withstand. It is the indwelling presence of ALMIGHTY GOD that empowers you to overcome any and every obstacle. He gives us power to bend and not break.

Secondly, the tree is not a fast grower; it takes time (some ten to forty years) for a tree to become fully-grown. So don't be in a hurry. Fast growth is not good growth; it takes time to build a life pleasing unto GOD. It's preparation before duty. Jesus said in [Matt. 7:5], "clean your own eye first, then you can help your brother see clearer". Be a billboard for GOD, a light that sits on a hill.

People will see your changed life as a witness before they hear your verbal witness.

Once the man was cleansed of the legion, the town folks came out to JESUS and the first thing they saw was he who had the legion, sitting and clothed and in his right mind [Mk. 5:15]. If you noticed, the changed man never spoke a word, his life spoke before he did it verbally. As a matter of fact, he never spoke to anybody but JESUS.

Again, let me remind you, a life pleasing to GOD takes time. The foundation for this GOD pleasing life has already been laid by GOD [1 Cor. 3:10-11], "For other foundation can no man lay than that is laid, which is Jesus Christ". David calls Him [2 Sam. 22:47; Ps. 89:26] "The rock of my salvation". This foundational rock has limitations. You can't build beyond specifications of the foundation; you can't use the blueprint of your own imagination, opinion or ideas of what the building should look like. That has already been predetermined/settled in the pre-council of Almighty GOD. [Rom. 8:29] "He also did predestinate to be conformed to the image of his Son".

Paul writes to the Colossians Christians [Col. 2:6] "As ye have therefore received Christ Jesus the

Lord, so walk ye in him"; the apostle John agrees [1 Jn. 2:6] "He that saith he abideth in him ought himself also so to walk, even as he walked" the word "walk" carries the idea of life or lifestyle. Since you received JESUS CHRIST as a model/blueprint with the hopes of pleasing GOD in instructions as to how to pattern or build your life, then do it continually, conducting yourselves with a conscience totally submissive to JESUS CHRIST'S LORDSHIP.

When we abide in The LORD JESUS, our lives take on the identity of the model. Notice what JESUS said in [Jn. 15:5], "I am the vine ye are the branches". The branches and the tree are one. The branches are identified by the tree. As you develop, you should begin looking like a lil' Jesus. The branches are non-existent without being groped in the tree. Paul used the word "rooted" in [Col. 2:7]. It is the metaphor of a tree whose roots runs deep and wide. The word "rooted", or "*rhidzo'-o*", means "to be stable"; we're not church hoppers neither are we tossed to and fro' by every wind of doctrine.

Every approaching wind is a test to our standing firm in the faith and determining that we will not be moved by such things. We are stable/committed, desiring and mediating next to "rivers of water". Notice "rivers" are plural referring to an overflowing supply; therefore, the most important part of a tree is the hidden root system that draws up water and nourishment such as the most important part of the believer's life is the "spiritual root system" that draws on the hidden resources we have in CHRIST. [Eph. 3:17 (amp)] "May Christ through your faith [actually] dwell (settle down, abide, make His permanent home) in your hearts! May you be rooted deep in love and founded securely on love", again, [Col. 2:7 (AMP)] "Have the roots [of your being] firmly and deeply planted [in Him, fixed and founded in Him], being continually built up in Him, becoming increasingly more confirmed and established in the faith, just as you were taught, and abounding and overflowing in it with thanksgiving".

Paul says everything we need is in JESUS: an overflowing of love, an overflowing of forgiveness, an overflowing of peace and joy unspeakable. "He's working in you" according to [Phil. 2:13] "both to will and to do of His good pleasure". You can't fail because there's no failure in GOD. Think about it! You're established, firmly rooted, have access to a refreshing river of blessings, and are tested genuine by the storms of life; but you will produce. "You will bring forth seasonal fruit". These fruits, according to the apostle Paul in [Gal. 5:22; Eph. 5:9], are "fruits of the Spirit" and proving what is acceptable unto the LORD.

Therefore, GOD's expectation in us is never a disappointment, because what's in Him is being transferred into you. However, it can't stay in you only because you are a channel; what you receive from Him, you must share with others. That's why we have love for the brothering and peace among ourselves. Paul says [Eph. 5:9] "For the fruit of the Spirit is in all goodness and righteousness and truth". "His leaf also shall not wither". In other words, your profession is backed up with faith and works; you're busy working because you are expecting something from GOD. You need to be like a tree; strong, steadfast, alive, beautiful, fruitful, useful and enduring. JESUS died on a tree, died just for you.

Be like a tree my beloved brother/sister, letting the light of GOD's glory radiate out of you through a changed life. Be like a tree when the winds of adversity blow hot against you. Bend but never break. Stand up for JESUS as He stood up for you. I close this session with steadfast words of the apostle Paul:

Romans 1:16-17 – "For I am not ashamed of the gospel of Christ: for it is the power of God unto salvation to everyone that believeth; to the Jew first, and also to the Greek. For therein is the righteousness of God revealed from faith to faith: as it is written, the just shall live by faith".

ABOUT THE AUTHOR

Pastor Louis Thomas has forty years of preaching, teaching, and ministering GOD'S word to many. He is the founder and presiding Pastor of the Bethlehem M.B.C., 1190 South Beech Street Picayune, Mississippi. He is a husband and father.

GOD has anointed and blessed him to touch hearts and minds to lead many to a better walk and understanding of GOD'S HOLY WORD.

Pastor Thomas is the former founder and radio Bible teacher of the program "A Few Crumbs from Bethlehem" and the organizer of the minister's fellowship group, "Iron Sharpens Iron".

ACKNOWLEDGMENT

A sincere thank you to Julie Keene for editing and publishing, for her professionalism and God given talents for bringing this work of GOD collected in this book alive.

Thank you, Rev. Carl Flowers, for your generous heart and genuine friendship. I thank GOD for you. I pray your ministry blossoms and you achieve all GOD has for you.

Thank you, Rev. John Guy, for your willingness to serve unselfishly. I believe GOD has blessed me with a fellow laborer. Remain faithful.

Thank you to every member of Bethlehem for your prayers, understanding hearts, and encouraging words as well as your unselfish willingness to share me with many. You are the best.

Thank you to all the pastors, ministers, laymen and women alike whose encouraging words motivated me to bring this book to a finished product.

www.ingramcontent.com/pod-product-compliance
Lightning Source LLC
Chambersburg PA
CBHW062011040426
42447CB00010B/2006